SONIA SOTOMAYOR

SUPREME COURT JUSTICE

by Carmen T. Bernier-Grand

illustrated by Thomas Gonzalez

MARSHALL CAVENDISH CHILDREN

ACKNOWLEDGMENTS

Mil gracias to

Eric Kimmel, Lisette Bernier-McGowan, Pat Ridgeway,

Fernando Comulada, Betsy Mays, and Tito Báez

Text copyright © 2010 by Carmen T. Bernier-Grand
Illustrations copyright © 2010 by Thomas Gonzalez

Library of Congress Cataloging-in-Publication Data

Bernier-Grand, Carmen T.
Sonia Sotomayor : Supreme Court Justice / by Carmen T. Bernier-Grand ;
illustrated by Thomas Gonzalez. — 1st ed.
p. cm.
ISBN 978-0-7614-5795-4
1. Sotomayor, Sonia, 1954—Juvenile literature. 2. Judges—United
States—Biography—Juvenile literature. 3. United States. Supreme
Court—Biography—Juvenile literature. I. Gonzalez, Thomas, 1959- II.
Title.
KF8745.S67B473 2010
347.73'2634—dc22
[B]
2009048363

The illustrations are rendered in mixed medium, pastels, technical pens, and airbrush.
Book design by Patrice Sheridan
Editor: Margery Cuyler
Printed in Malaysia (T)
First edition
1 3 5 6 4 2

Marshall Cavendish
Children

To the mothers of the universe

—C.T.B·G

To my wife Noni and my daughter Nina;
thanks for your constant support in everything I do

—T.G.

AS AMERICAN AS MANGO PIE

Sonia is Greek for "wisdom,"
profound knowledge,
prudent conduct.

On June 25, 1954,
Sonia Sotomayor is born
to Puerto Rican parents,
Juan Luis Sotomayor
and Celina Báez de Sotomayor,
in *Nueva* York.
Sonia Sotomayor is a Nuyorican,
as American as mango pie.

RIDING HER TRICYCLE
IN BRONXDALE

When Sonia is three, her brother,
Juan Luis Sotomayor Jr., is born.
The new baby is nicknamed Junior.
His parents say he's tranquil,
but tranquil his sister Sonia is not.

The day the family moves to Bronxdale,
a housing project in the South Bronx,
Sonia speeds on her tricycle,
screeches to a halt,
and scrapes a freshly painted wall.

No, tranquil Sonia is not.

MAMI: CELINA BÁEZ DE SOTOMAYOR

Born in 1927 in Lajas, Puerto Rico.
Mami, age nine, watches her mother die.
Her father abandons his five children.
Mami's sister Aurora raises them.
Mami, age seventeen,
joins the Women's Army Auxiliary Corps,
trains in Georgia, serves in Manhattan,
marries *Papi*, finishes high school,
has two children, Sonia and Junior.

Mami, age thirty-five,
carries breakfast to a sick neighbor,
takes his temperature and blood pressure,
returns home to cook *arroz con habichuelas*,
leaves the pot on the stove in case her kids come home hungry,
hustles them out to Blessed Sacrament School,
sends the monthly payment for *Encyclopedia Britannica*,
heads out to Prospect Hospital, where she answers phones,
announces on the intercom, "Bring down the sheets."
The "ee" comes out as "i."
Mami's boss keeps her off the switchboard,
sends her to a six-month course in practical nursing.
Mami yearns to be a registered nurse.

PAPI: JUAN LUIS SOTOMAYOR

Born in 1921 in Santurce, Puerto Rico.
In third grade, *Papi* drops out of school.

A heart defect keeps him out of the army.
He moves to Manhattan during World War II.

Papi is a highly skilled worker.

He makes tools that cut, shape, and form metal.

Papi is a terrific cook!
He makes the best *mofongo* in the South Bronx.

Papi doesn't speak English;
Sonia speaks to him in Spanish.

He takes Sonia to Yankee Stadium
to watch the Yankees play.

When "The Star-Spangled Banner" is sung,
they stand and place their right hands over their hearts.

Eating frankfurters with ketchup,
Papi teaches Sonia the rules of baseball.

When a Yankee hits a home run,
Papi tosses his cap into the sky.
¡*Wepa!*

¡wepa!

PLAYING BINGO IN BRONXDALE

Sonia marks the last empty square with a chick pea.
"Bingo!" she calls.
Junior's mouth bends out of shape.
His sister has won again!
Cousins Mili, Eddie, and Nelson slide their chick peas
onto the table to start a new game.
Sonia is as hungry as a barracuda.
Papi is cooking pigs' feet with *garbanzos*,
simmering till tender.
Titi Carmen, *Titi* Gloria, and *Mami*
offer goat cheese topped with sweet guava paste.
Their heads, feet, and hips dance
to the rhythm of the *merengue*
the record player plays.
Papi clicks two dominos to the tune.
"*¡Eh-eh-ah! Palo bonito palo es.*"
The dominos on the table look like
the buildings in Bronxdale,
core of Sonia's universe.

VACATIONING IN
PUERTO RICO

The island family waits at the
San Juan airport.
A commotion of hugs and kisses.

Their cars, packed like subway cars,
caravan to Mayagüez.
Zebu bulls switch their tails as the cars pass.

In Mayagüez, barefoot Sonia buys a cranberry *piragua*,
its crushed ice pyramid topped with sweet syrupy tamarind.

At Boquerón Beach, a sea wave gives Sonia a ride
on its *mundillo*-lace skirt; returns her to sun-bleached sand.

When the sky starts to rust, porch voices tell family stories.
Sonia plays jacks with her cousins.

Hundreds, no, thousands of tree frogs sing, *"Kokee-kokee!"*
They lull Sonia to sleep.

When she returns to New York, she can't sleep
without the *kokee-kokee-kokees.*

NO SWEETS

Sonia—
woozy, sleepy, hungry, thirsty.
¡Ay! The doctor pricks her finger
with a tiny needle;
squeezes it.
Blood squirts out.

Sonia has diabetes.
What's that? What does it mean?
    No more *piraguas*. No more guava paste.
    Sonia has to learn to give herself insulin shots.
    Every day. A shot in her belly.
    Why can't she be like any other third grader?

No guava

¡no!

piraguas

READING IN ENGLISH

Sonia's fingertips trace each word.
Maybe her teacher won't call on her.
The teacher calls.
Sonia reads, "Chark."
"Shark," the teacher corrects.
No "sh" sound in Spanish.
Sonia's shameful secret:
Words in English have no meaning.

GRIEVING FOR *PAPI*

Papi is dead.
People say he died *de repente*,
as if *de repente* ("suddenly")
    is some kind of sickness.
Papi died of a heart attack.
Titi Gloria tells Junior and Sonia
that *Papito Dios* took *Papi* to *el cielo*.
She means heaven, but *cielo* also is sky.
Sonia imagines *Papi* floating in the sky
    like Casper the friendly ghost.

Tías, dressed like black crows, fly from Puerto Rico.
Their wings flap around Sonia. "¡Ay, *bendito!*"
    They whisper long rosary litanies:
    "Holy Mary, pray for us."
Ribbons and glittering names on floral wreaths float by *Papi's* coffin.
    Papi is cold. He needs a blanket.
Mami seizes Junior by his wrist, squeezes Sonia's left hand.
    Trik-trak. Trik-trak. Trik-trak.
Their slow funeral steps follow the coffin to the cemetery.

IN *NUEVA* YORK WITH HER *TÍAS*

Titi Carmen takes Sonia and Junior to Yankee Stadium.
Sonia sits on a spot on the bleachers
still warm with memories of *Papi.*
Because of him, she's a die-hard baseball fan.
Because of him, she loves the Yankees.

Titi Gloria takes them to see *El circo*
starring the Mexican comedian Cantinflas.
They come in late; see the end half of the movie.
They stay and see the first half.
They do not see the movie from beginning to end.

UNDERSTANDING STORIES

What clicked?
Sonia doesn't know.
In fifth grade, she starts to understand
the stories she reads in English.

A NUYORICAN NANCY DREW

Mami has to work two jobs.
When *Abuelita* can't take care of Sonia and Junior,
the children have to go to the garment factory with *Titi* Gloria.
   Monstrous sewing machines crank up,
   windows grow black.
   Fresh air, please.

Sonia lends Junior her *Casper* and *Archie* comics.
She buries herself in *Nancy Drew* books,
dreams of becoming a detective, like Nancy.
Follow clues. Catch criminals.
Sonia watches *Perry Mason*,
dreams of becoming a lawyer, like Perry.
Fight crime. Fight injustice.
Bring law and order to the streets.

WORKING WEEKENDS AND SUMMERS

At fourteen,
Saturdays, Sundays, summers,
Sonia
mops floors at *Titi* Carmen's store.
Scrapes pastry pans at a bakery.
Cleans slops in offices.
But never after school.
After-school time is for studying.

STUDYING AT HOME

A nun orders boys and girls to the opposite wings
of Cardinal Spellman High School.
After school, Kevin, Mili, Sergio, and Ken go
to Sonia's house to use the *Encyclopedia Britannica*,
the only encyclopedia in Co-op City,
where Sonia now lives.
Sonia doesn't let Junior go out into the streets.
Too many losses.
This month a Puerto Rican died in the Vietnam War,
and last month and more next month.
In a slow, deep, and patient voice,
Sonia speaks of those who return
from war without a right hand to shake.
She palms the table to make her point.
Impressed by her speech on the senseless war,
Ken urges her to apply to Princeton University,
where he'll go the following year.
"You'll receive a full scholarship," he tells her.
Sonia laughs.
"The only thing I know about Ivy League schools
is the movie *Love Story*."

STUDYING WITH *MAMI*

Mami is home!

Sonia and Junior hug her, kiss her. "*Bendición.*"

"*Que Dios me los bendiga*", *Mami* answers.

Drinking *café puya*, no sugar, no milk,

Sonia talks about Princeton University.

"Do whatever you want," *Mami* answers,

"but do it well and with pride."

Besides working two jobs,

Mami is studying to be a registered nurse.

Mami, Junior, and Sonia study until after midnight.

Then Sonia goes to her side of the master bedroom.

Junior goes to the other side, a curtain between them.

Mami sleeps in the smaller bedroom—if she sleeps.

At dawn, Sonia finds *Mami* still studying.

"I am half the woman she is."

20

LEARNING TO WRITE IN ENGLISH

"Social isolation is going to be part of your experience,"
Ken warns Sonia when she gets to Princeton University.
"You have to have strength of character to get through intact."
    Sonia's first history essay
    is returned to her bloody,
    comments and corrections in red.
    She can barely write a college paper!
    She hides in her dorm room.
Shall Sonia return home?

Mami is excelling in school.
She'll graduate as a registered nurse soon.
Sonia can't disappoint *Mami*.
"I am all I am because of her."
Elementary school books out,
Sonia practices her grammar,
attends writing classes,
reads classics:
    Huckleberry Finn
    Alice in Wonderland
    Pride and Prejudice
She barricades herself in the library
until she finally conquers writing.

STUDENT RIGHTS

No Latino professors,
no Latino administrators,
too few women students
fewer yet Latino students
at Princeton University.
In her sophomore year,
Sonia visits the office of the president of Princeton.
"What good is it to know what happens in the Ural Mountains of Russia
if you don't know what is happening a few miles around you?"
Cold reaction. Some words. No action.
Sonia files a complaint accusing Princeton
of discrimination in hiring and admission.
"Words are transitory;
it is the practice of the ideas you espouse
that affect society and are permanent."
Princeton hires a Latino administrator,
    invites a Puerto Rican to teach.
        Sonia herself recruits minority students.
            "Princeton changed us, not just academically,
                but also in what we learned about life
                and the world.

            At the same time, we changed
            Princeton."

MARRYING KEVIN

In June 1976 Sonia graduates *summa cum laude* from Princeton. She marries her high-school boyfriend, Kevin E. Noonan, in a chapel at Saint Patrick's Cathedral. "I don't want children," Mrs. Sonia Sotomayor de Noonan says. "Being diabetic has something to do with it—there are potential health risks. But then, there are plenty of diabetic women who happily take the risk. I suppose I am just personally too selfish about my life, about myself. I don't think I could freely devote the kind of attention to a child that a child needs." Her career is her life. Sonia is a law student at Yale University; Kevin is a graduate student at Princeton. They grow apart. They divorce after seven years.

DREAMING TRUE DREAMS

The Princeton student who couldn't write well
is now the editor of the *Yale Law Journal*.
After graduating as a lawyer from Yale Law School,
   Sonia works at the Manhattan District Attorney's Office,
prosecuting street crimes—
   pickpocketing, car thefts, vandalism.
Five years later,
   Sonia joins the law firm of Pavia & Harcourt.
When investigating counterfeiters,
   Sonia wears a bulletproof vest,
fulfilling her Nancy Drew dreams.

TOUCHING THE SKY

1991

Is the year Sonia's firm partner urges her to apply to be a federal judge.

Is the year Sonia turns thirty-seven, too young for the seat.

   "They will not even consider me."

Is the year President George H.W. Bush nominates Sonia to be a federal judge
   in the Southern District of New York.

1992

Is the year Sonia is easily confirmed.

Is the year she leaves behind a hefty income, a view of Manhattan,
   and Italian paintings
     for the excitement of wearing judicial robes.

Is the year the court announces her name as the first Nuyorican federal judge.

   "I feel I can touch the sky."

SIGNING HER FIRST CONVICTION

Alone in her office,
Sonia signs her first conviction.
She is sending
a Nuyorican
drug offender
from the projects
to five years in prison.
He could have been her or Junior—
if it hadn't been for *Mami*.

A HOME RUN FROM THE BENCH

"You can't grow up in the South Bronx
   without knowing about baseball."
         "Judge! Judge!"
               Bronxdale friends call out at Yankee Stadium.
                  Sonia sits with them on the bleachers.
Baseball players go on strike,
   protesting the owners' new rules.
         First time in ninety years without a World Series!
            Baseball will be ruined for all.
On March 30, 1995,
   Judge Sotomayor presides over the hearing.
         She scolds the owners for unfair labor practices.
            "One side can't come up with new rules
                  unless they negotiate with the other side."
She urges both sides to salvage the 1995 season,
   reach new labor agreements, change their attitude.
         Sonia saves baseball.

TAKING AN OATH OF LOVE

In 1997, President Bill Clinton nominates Sonia to be promoted
to judge of the Court of Appeals of the Second Circuit in New York.
Some senators look for a "gotcha!"
  "She's a woman. She's Latina. She's Catholic.
  She must be a bleeding-heart liberal."
The Senate postpones the vote.
Sonia waits, waits with a man she loves, Peter White.
In October 1998, almost a year after her nomination,
Sonia is finally confirmed.
"I have never perceived myself as poor
because I have been rich
in the most important things in life,
the love, affection, and support of family, friends,
and sometimes even strangers."
To her fiancé she says,
"Peter, you have made me
a whole person, filling not just the voids
of emptiness that existed before you,
but making me a better, a more loving
and more generous person."
He helps her put on the black judicial robe.

NOT THE SAME LUCK

Sonia presides
over the marriage of *Mami* to Omar López.
Omar brings *Mami* romance and happiness.
Sonia doesn't have *Mami's* luck.
Peter prefers wood trails and lakes
to the power-walking trail of the Brooklyn Bridge,
the coal brick oven of Grimaldi's Pizzeria,
the sausages at Joe's Dairy,
Yankee Stadium games, Broadway plays,
American Ballet Theater, the Metropolitan Opera House—
the dazzling New York City Sonia loves.

Peter buys a small boat, navigates the lakes in upstate New York,
marries a woman fourteen years younger than Sonia,
a woman Sonia knows.

GOLDILOCKS IN CRIMINAL COURT

"I made it. So can you,"
Sonia tells high school students.
"You just have to work hard."
She and her lawyer friends
teach them how to speak, how to dress,
how to be lawyers.
They run a mock trial.

Goldilocks is charged with burglary,
entering and remaining in the three bears' home,
stealing their porridge, breaking their chairs.

The students write scripts, play the roles
of prosecutors, defenders, jurors;
bring the case before Judge Sotomayor.
Is Goldilocks guilty or not guilty?

"WHO AM I?"

On May 26, 2009, in the East Room of the White House
President Barack Obama announces Sonia as his pick to the Supreme Court.
He calls her "an inspiring woman"
with an "extraordinary journey."
Mami and Junior, now Dr. Juan Luis Sotomayor,
are present when Sonia says,

"I stand on the shoulders of countless people,
yet there's an extraordinary person who is my life's inspiration.
That person is my mother, Celina Sotomayor."

The hearings begin. Senators test Sonia with questions.
Palming the table gently,
she answers in a slow, deep voice.
Some senators are not satisfied with her answers.
Will Sonia be confirmed? Will the process last a year again?
Senators ask for an extra week to consider the nomination.
Mami waits. Junior waits. Sonia waits.

"Who am I? I am a Nuyorican,
a born and bred New Yorker
raised by Puerto Rican parents."
On August 6, 2009, the Senate votes.

Sonia Sotomayor,
as American as mango pie,
is the first Latina Justice
to be elected to the Supreme Court
of the United States.

THE EXTRAORDINARY JOURNEY OF JUSTICE SONIA SOTOMAYOR

"If you spend more time applying yourself
than worrying about outcomes,
you are bound to get a lot farther."

Sonia Sotomayor was born in New York City on June 25, 1954. Her father, Juan Luis Sotomayor, was a tool and die maker from Santurce, Puerto Rico. Her mother, Celina Báez de Sotomayor, was a telephone operator and later a nurse from Lajas, Puerto Rico.

When Sonia was three, her brother Juan (Junior) was born, and the family moved to Bronxdale, a housing project for low-income people in the South Bronx. Her grandmother and some of her uncles, aunts, and cousins lived nearby and visited often.

Sonia was eight when she was diagnosed with childhood diabetes. She had to learn to inject herself with insulin. She jokes that people in the projects thought her mother gave the best shots. Sonia begs to differ.

Celina Sotomayor was planning to return to nursing school in September 1963, but in April her husband had a heart attack and died. Celina had to set her dreams aside and work two jobs—six days a week.

Although Celina couldn't afford to send her children to private schools, she managed to scrape together enough money to buy them the *Encyclopedia Britannica*. Celina believed in the importance of a good education and pushed her children to study hard.

Sonia could read English aloud but couldn't comprehend it. It wasn't until fifth grade that she began to understand what she read. Suddenly the world opened up to her. She dreamed of traveling and becoming a detective, like Nancy Drew.

During Sonia's first year at Cardinal Spellman High School, the boys and girls were segregated in opposite wings of the school, but by the time Sonia graduated as the valedictorian, the nuns had dropped that rule. It was in high school that Sonia met Kevin Noonan. They were married right after she graduated from Princeton in 1976. They divorced seven years later, perhaps because Sonia, who still struggled with diabetes, did not think they should have children. They were also very busy, too busy to spend much time together.

Sonia has remarked that Princeton was like an alien land to her. She had not gotten the education or travel experience her classmates had. But she knew that if she dropped out, her mother would be very disappointed. After Sonia's junior year in high school, Celina Sotomayor had attended Hostos Community College to become a registered nurse. If she could work hard to achieve her goals, so could Sonia. At Princeton, Sonia buckled down and studied hard. Joining the groups *Acción Puertorriqueña* and Third World Center kept her from becoming too isolated. After four years of strenuous academic work and extracurricular activities, she received the Moses Taylor Pyne Prize her senior year. She wrote her senior thesis on the first elected governor of Puerto Rico, Don Luis Muñoz Marín. She graduated with a *Phi Beta Kappa* key and *summa cum laude* with a BA in history.

After Princeton, Sonia attended Yale Law School and became the editor of the *Yale Law Journal*. At a recruiting dinner, lawyers at a Washington law firm suggested that she had been accepted to attend Yale only because of affirmative action. Sonia filed a complaint. A faculty-student tribunal was formed to decide if the law firm should be barred from recruiting on campus. Two of the three white male faculty members sided with the firm, but the students backed Sonia, and the law firm was forced to apologize.

In June 1979, Sonia graduated from Yale as a lawyer. Meanwhile her brother, Juan, graduated from the City University of New York's Sophie Davis School of Biomedical Education at City College. (Today he's an allergy and asthma doctor near Syracuse, New York.)

After law school, Sonia worked as an assistant district attorney in Manhattan and served as associate, then partner, at the New York law firm Pavia & Harcourt.

In 1991, Senator Daniel Patrick Moynihan recommended her, and President George H.W. Bush nominated her, for the federal bench. She was easily confirmed.

Legend has it that Sonia saved baseball. On March 30, 1995, she issued an injunction against baseball team owners, ending a seven-month strike that had cancelled the World Series for the first time in ninety years.

Around this time Sonia met Peter White, a contractor in Brooklyn. Even though they both grew up in the Bronx, they did not have much in common. He loved the country. She loved New York City. Still, they became engaged.

In 1997, President Bill Clinton tapped her for a spot as a judge on the federal appeals court. Fearing that Sonia was too liberal and that she was Clinton's candidate for the Supreme Court, the U.S. Senate delayed the vote for a year.

The day Sonia was confirmed, her fiancé, Peter White, helped her put on the black robe. But just after Sonia's fiftieth birthday, Peter left her for a woman fourteen years her junior.

Some people describe Sonia as a bully at the bench. But many others defend her, saying that she cannot tolerate lawyers who come to the courtroom unprepared. She works hard and sticks closely to the law when deciding a case. She expects everyone else to work hard, too. Her staff says that she invites them to Christmas parties and that she's a devoted godmother to many of their children.

In 2009 there had only been two women appointed to the Supreme Court—and no Latino had ever been a Justice. But on May 26, 2009, President Barack Obama nominated Sonia Sotomayor for the Supreme Court.

"I can't feel my body," her mother said after the announcement. "That's how proud I am of her."

On August 6, 2009, the Senate voted 68 to 31 to confirm Sonia as the 111th justice. Two days later, with her mother holding the Bible and her brother at her side, Sonia Sotomayor took the oath as the first Hispanic Justice in the high court of the United States of America.

GLOSSARY

Arroz con habichuelas: Rice and beans

¡Ay!: Ouch!

¡Ay, bendito!: A Puerto Rican saying that expresses sadness

Bendición: Blessings

Café puya: Black coffee without sugar

Cantinflas: The Mexican comedian, Alfonso Mario Moreno Reyes

"¡Eh-eh-ah! Palo bonito palo es": Lyrics of the song "Palo bonito," or "Beautiful Tree"

"El circo": "The Circus"

Ivy League: An association of eight universities and colleges in the northeastern United States: Brown, Columbia, Cornell, Dartmouth, Harvard, Princeton, the University of Pennsylvania, and Yale

Lajas: A quiet valley town in the western part of Puerto Rico where Sonia's mother was born

Mami: Mommy

Mayagüez: The third-largest city in Puerto Rico

Merengue: A type of music that originated in the Dominican Republic

Mofongo: Smashed plantains flavored with garlic, salt, and olive oil

Mundillo: A type of lace

Nueva York: New York

Nuyorican: A person born in New York to Puerto Rican parents

Papi: Daddy

Papito Dios: Little Father God

Piragua: Snow cone

Que Dios me los bendiga: May God bless you

Santurce: A vicinity in San Juan, the capital of Puerto Rico

Tías: Aunts

Titi: Auntie

¡Wepa!: Hooray!

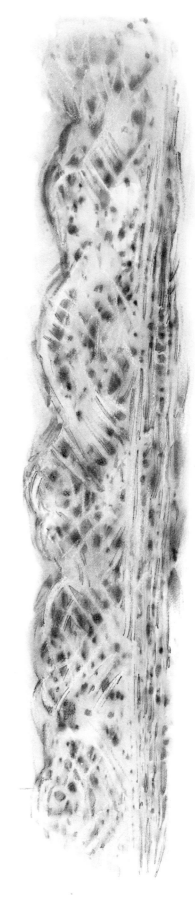

CHRONOLOGY

1954—On June 25, Sonia Sotomayor is born in New York City.

1957—Sonia's brother, Juan Luis Sotomayor Jr., is born. The family moves to Bronxdale, a low-income housing project in the South Bronx.

1962—Sonia is diagnosed with Type I diabetes.

1963—Sonia's father, Juan Luis Sotomayor Sr., dies of a heart attack at age forty-two.

1972—In June, Sonia graduates from Cardinal Spellman High School as class valedictorian. In September, she enters Princeton University.

1973—Sonia's mother graduates from the nursing program at the City University of New York's Hostos Community College.

1976—Sonia is awarded the Moses Taylor Pyne Prize for her excellent grades and extracurricular activities. Her senior thesis is on the first elected governor of Puerto Rico, Don Luis Muñoz Marín. In June, she graduates with a *Phi Beta Kappa* key and *summa cum laude*, with a BA in history. On August 14, she marries her high-school boyfriend, Kevin Edward Noonan.

1979—In June, Sonia graduates a Juris Doctor from Yale Law School after serving as editor of the *Yale Law Journal*. Sonia's brother graduates from the City University of New York's Sophie Davis School of Biomedical Education at City College.

1979-1984—Sonia is an assistant district attorney in the office of the District Attorney of New York, New York City, prosecuting felonies.

1983—Sonia and Kevin Noonan get divorced.

1984-1987—Sonia is an associate at Pavia & Harcourt.

1988-1992—Sonia is a partner at Pavia & Harcourt.

1991—In November, President George H.W. Bush nominates Sonia to serve as a federal judge for the U.S. District Court, Southern District of New York.

1992—On August 11, the U.S. Senate confirms Sonia as a federal judge.

1995—On March 31, Sonia issues an injunction against baseball team owners, ending a seven-and-a-half-month strike that had forced cancellation of the World Series for the first time in ninety years.

1997—President William J. Clinton nominates Sonia to serve as a judge for the U.S. Court of Appeals for the Second Circuit in New York.

1998–2007—Sonia is an adjunct professor at New York University School of Law.

1998—Sonia becomes engaged to Peter White, a contractor, in New York City. On October 2, she is inducted into the U.S. District Court of Appeals for the Second Circuit.

1998–2009—Sonia serves as an appellate judge.

1999–2009—Sonia is a lecturer at Columbia Law School.

2000—Sonia and Peter White separate.

2009—On May 26, President Barack Obama nominates Judge Sonia Sotomayor to the Supreme Court. On August 6, the Senate confirms Justice Sonia Sotomayor. On August 8, Sonia Sotomayor takes the oath of office.

SOURCES

Abanet.org. "National Hispanic Heritage Month 2000," American Library Association, October 2000. <www.abanet.org/publiced/Hispanics.html>.

ABCNews. "Life of Sonia Sotomayor," May 2009.

Beck, Joe. "Sonia Sotomayor Reflects on Her Success," The Hispanic Outlook, March 27, 2003.

Becker, Jo and David Gonzalez. "Sotomayor, a Trailblazer and a Dreamer," *The New York Times*, May 26, 2009. <www.nytimes.com/2009/05/27/us/politics/27websotomayor.html>.

Bernier-Grand, Carmen. Interview with José Alberto (*Tito*) Báez. Tito's Bakery, Mayagüez, Puerto Rico, July 28, 2009.

Bort, Ina R. "Hon. Sonia Sotomayor: U.S. Circuit Judge, U.S. Court of Appeals for Second District," *The Federal Lawyer*, February 2006.

Carson, Nancy. *Believing in Yourselves*. Kansas City: Andrew McMeel Publishing, 2002.

Falcón, Angelo. "Sonia Sotomayor as American as Mango Pie," <www.CNN.com>, July 3, 2009.

Graglia, Diego. "Pride of Sonia Sotomayor Reflected in Spanish-Language Media," May 27, 2009. <http://feetin2worlds.wordpress.com>.

Kantor, Jodi and David Gonzalez. "For Sotomayor and Thomas, Paths Fork at Race and Identity," *The New York Times*, Sunday, June 7, 2009.

Kellman, Laurie. "Sotomayor Tastes: Pig Innards, 'Law & Order'." *The Associated Press*, June 5, 2009.

Lacayo, Richard. "Sonia Sotomayor: A Justice Like No Other," *Time Magazine*, May 28, 1009, <www.time.com/time/nation/article/0,8599,1901348,00.html>.

Lawton, Catherine. "A Touch of Class," *Mademoiselle*, September 1986.

López Cabán, Cynthia. "*Sería un regalo maravilloso*," *El Nuevo Día*, May 2, 2009.

Mulero, Leonor. "*Una carrera judicial llena de logros*," *El Nuevo Día*, December 23, 1998.

Nicholas, Peter and James Oliphant. "Sonia Sotomayor: Two Sides of a Life," *The Swamp*, May 31, 2009.

Nieves Ramírez, Gladys. "*Orgullo de la jueza en Mayagüez*," *El Nuevo Día*, December 23, 1998.

NYtimes.com <www.video.on.nytimes.com/2009/06/10/politics/>.

Sanchez-Korrol, Virginia. "Mentoring Sonia: The Case of Celina Sotomayor," Huffington Post, <www.huffingtonpost.com/virginia-sanchexkorrol/ mentoring-sonia-the-case-of-celina-sotomayor>.

Smith, Greg B. "Judge's Journey to Top," New York: *Daily News*, October 24, 1998.

Sotomayor, Sonia. Mario G. Olmos Memorial Lecture; "A Latina Judge's Voice," delivered at the University of California School of Law in 2001 and published in *Berkeley La Raza Law Journal*, Spring 2002 issue.

Sotomayor, Sonia. "Letter to the Editor: Anti-Latino Discrimination at Princeton," *The Daily Princetonian*, May 10, 1974.

Powell, Michael, Russ Buettner, and Serge F. Kovaleski. "To Get to Sotomayor's Core, Start in New York," *The New York Times*, July 10, 2009.

Tedford, Deborah. "Obama Chooses Sotomayor for Supreme Court," NPR, June 24, 2009.

Time.com. "How Sotomayor 'Saved' Baseball," <www.time.com/time/nation/ article/0,8599,1900974,00.html>.

Vega, María. "*Frentes y perfiles de una jueza*," *El Diario La Prensa*, October 10, 1998, United States Senate Hearing. July 14–16, 2009.

White House. "Background on Judge Sonia Sotomayor," May 26, 2009.

NOTES

As American as Mango Pie

As American as mango pie: Falcón, Angelo, "Sonia Sotomayor as American as Mango Pie"

Riding a Tricycle in Bronxdale

Bronxdale Houses: A 28-building, seven-story public housing project in the South Bronx.

Mami: Celina Báez de Sotomayor

Celina's sister: Aurora lived with them in New York City.

Women's Army Auxiliary Corps (WAAC): 150,000 American women who served in World War II. They were the first women other than nurses to serve in the army.

"Bring down the sheets.": www.video.on.nytimes.com/2009/06/10/politics/.

Papi: Juan Luis Sotomayor

Papi: While *Mami* finished high school, *Papi* worked as a truck driver.

Playing Bingo in Bronxdale

Cousins: Milagros Báez O'Toole, Eddie and Nelson Sotomayor.

Vacationing in Puerto Rico

Cousins: Irma, Rosa, Mario, Eva Leonor and José Alberto (*Tito*) Báez.

In *Nueva* York with her *Tías*

Movies: The Brook Avenue Theater showed movies in Spanish.

A Nuyorican Nancy Drew

Mami's two jobs: Telephone operator and practical nurse at Prospect Hospital in the Bronx. Later, as a registered nurse, she worked at the Velez Mental Health Clinic.

Perry Mason: No doubt Sonia noticed that some episodes had women judges.

Working Weekends and Summers

Titi Carmen: This aunt had a clothing store in Hunts Point in the Bronx.

Studying at Home

Opposite wings: The nuns made the classrooms co-ed while Sonia was attending Cardinal Spellman High School.

Mili: Milagros Báez O'Toole is Sonia's cousin.

Ken: Kenneth Moy, son of Chinese immigrants, was a year ahead of Sonia.

Sergio: Cuban Sergio Sotolongo was a year behind Sonia at Cardinal Spellman High School and then at Princeton.

Kevin: Kevin Edward Noonan was Sonia's boyfriend. He graduated from Princeton with a PhD in microbiology and with a Juris Doctorate from the John Marshall Law School. Currently, he represents clients from biomedical and biotechnology companies.

Co-op City: At this point Sonia and her family lived in Co-op City, a 35-building community for middle-income families situated in the Bronx.

Studying with *Mami*

Mami: When Sonia was a junior in high school, Celina Sotomayor went to the City University of New York's Hostos Community College to get her registered nurse license.

"I am half the woman . . .": "The Life of Sonia Sotomayor."

Learning to Write in English

". . . social isolation . . .": Becker, "Sotomayor, a Trailblazer and a Dreamer."

Ken: Kenneth Moy is a lawyer in Oakland, California.

History class: Professor Nancy Weiss Malkiel tutored Sonia in reading and how to write analytically. She says that by the end of the year, Sonia was flourishing.

"I am all I am because of her.": "The Life of Sonia Sotomayor," ABC News.

Student Rights

"What good . . .": Sotomayor, "Letter to the Editor: Anti-Latino Discrimination at Princeton."

"Words are transitory. . . .": Ibid.

"Princeton changed us . . .": Beck, "Sonia Sotomayor Reflects in Her Success."

Marrying Kevin

"I don't want children . . .": Lawton, "A Touch of Class," p. 322. She has no children, but she's devoted to her nephews, Conner and Corey Sotomayor, and niece, Kylie Sotomayor. She's also the godmother of many children whose parents have worked for her.

Dreaming True Dreams

Prosecuting crimes: Sonia worked at the Manhattan District Attorney's Office.

Law firm: Pavia & Harcourt.

Touching the Sky

Partner: Managing litigation partner David A. Botwinick.

"They will not even consider me . . .": Abanet.org "National Hispanic Heritage Month 2000."

Vote: 68 yes, 28 no.

"I feel I can touch the sky:" www.nytimes.com/videos.

A Home Run from the Bench

"You can't grow up . . .": *Time Magazine.* "How Sotomayor 'Saved' Baseball," p. 1.

"Judge . . .": Becker. "Sotomayor, a Trailblazer and a Dreamer," p. 6.

"One side can't come up with new rules . . .": *Time Magazine.* "How Sotomayor 'Saved' Baseball," pp. 1–2.

Taking an Oath of Love

"She's a woman . . .": Smith, "Judge's Journey to Top."

"I have never perceived myself as poor . . .": Carson, *Believing in Yourselves,* p. 27.

"Peter, you have made me . . .": Michael Powell, "To Get to Sotomayor's Core," p. A16.

Not the Same Luck

Omar López: An Argentinian, Omar worked at an auto parts store. He and *Mami* now live in a retirement community in Margate, Florida.

Goldilocks in Criminal Court

Goldilocks: The Development School for Youth, an after-school program, introduces inner-city students to life in the professional world over twelve weeks.

"I made it . . .": U.S. Senate Hearings, July 15, 2009.

"Who Am I?"

Junior: Juan Luis Sotomayor Jr. is an allergy and asthma doctor in Syracuse, New York. He's married to Tracey Sotomayor. They have three children—Conner, Corey, and Kylie.

". . . an inspiring woman . . .": Tedford, "Obama Chooses Sotomayor for Supreme Court," p. 1.

". . . extraordinary journey . . .": Lacayo, "Sonia Sotomayor: A Justice Like No Other," p. 2.

"I stand on the shoulders . . .": "The Life of Sonia Sotomayor," ABC News.

"Who am I?" Sotomayor, "Lecture: 'A Latina Judge's Voice'."

The Extraordinary Journey of Justice Sonia Sotomayor

"If you spend . . .": Carson, *Believing in Yourselves,* p. 21.

"I can't feel my body . . .": Graglia, "Pride of Sonia Sotomayor Reflected in Spanish-Language Media."